CLASS ANIMA

Reptiles

Sarah Wilkes

WAYLAND

CLASSIFYING ANIMALS

Titles in this series:

Amphibians Birds Fish Insects Mammals Reptiles

Conceived and produced for Hodder Wayland by

Nutshell
MEDIA

www.nutshellmedialtd.co.uk

Consultant: Jane Mainwaring, Natural History Museum
Editor: Polly Goodman
Designer: Tim Mayer
Illustrator: Jackie Harland
Picture research: Morgan Interactive Ltd and Victoria Coombs

Published in Great Britain in 2006 by Hodder Wayland, an imprint of Hodder Children's Books.

This paperback edition published in 2007 by Wayland, an imprint of Hachette Children's Books.

British Library Cataloguing in Publication Data
Wilkes, Sarah, 1964-
Reptiles. – (Classifying animals)
1. Reptiles. – Classification – Juvenile literature
I. Title
597.9'012

ISBN 978 0 7502 5298 0

Cover photograph: close-up of iguana's yellow eye.
Title page (clockwise from top left): mangrove snake; Jackson's chameleon; Morelet's crocodile; Pacific turtle hatchling.
Chapter openers (from top to bottom): the skins of a Nile crocodile, an emerald tree boa, a rattlesnake and a marine iguana.

Picture acknowledgements
Corbis cover (Bryan F Peterson); **Ecoscene** 7 bottom, 8 (Reinhard Dirscheri), 9 (Jack Milchanowski), 10 (Wayne Lawler), 17 (Jack Milchanowski), 22 (Clive Druett), 28 (Robert Pickett), 35 (Reinhard Dirscheri), 43 (Alexandra Elliott Jones); **naturepl.com** 4 (Doug Wechsler), 5 (Steven David Miller), 7 top, 11 top (Jurgen Freund), 11 bottom (Michael Durham), 12 (Pete Oxford), 14 (Mike Wilkes), 15 (Tony Phelps), 16 (Nick Garbutt), 18 (George McCarthy), 19 (Mark Carwardine), 20 (Mary McDonald), 21 (Brandon Cole), 23 (John Cancalosi), 24 (Bruce Davidson), 25 (Michael Pitts), 26 (Stephen David Miller), 27 (Bruce Davidson), 29 (Nick Garbutt), 30 (Robert Valentic), 31 (Barry Mansell), 32 (David Kjaer), 33 (Tony Phelps), 34 (William Osborn), 36, 37 (Anup Shah), 38 (Bruce Davidson), 39, 40 (Anup Shah), 41 (Hermann Brehm), 42 (Bruce Davidson).

Printed and bound in China.

Hachette Children's Books
338 Euston Road, London NW1 3BH

CONTENTS

It is not possible to cover all the reptile families in this book. However, there is a complete list of the families, superfamilies, suborders and orders on page 44.

WHAT ARE REPTILES?

HUNDREDS OF MILLIONS OF YEARS AGO THE EARTH WAS ruled by reptiles – dinosaurs on the land, pterosaurs in the air and plesiosaurs in the sea. Most died out about 65 million years ago, but some survived. Today there are about 7,800 species of reptiles, including snakes, lizards, turtles and crocodiles.

Reptilian features

All reptiles share certain features by which they can be identified. Their body is covered in a continuous layer of scales that forms their leathery skin. These scales are different from the individual scales covering the bodies of fish. Their scaly skin helps to reduce water loss and has enabled reptiles to survive in desert habitats. Reptiles have a lower jaw made up of a series of bones, unlike mammals, which have a single jawbone. Like amphibians and birds, reptiles have a single bone in their middle ear, whereas mammals have three.

The scales covering snakes such as this mangrove snake (*Boiga dendrophila*) vary in size. They tend to be larger on the underside of the body and smaller on the upper surface.

All reptiles are ectothermic, or cold-blooded, which means that their body temperature is similar to their surroundings. They gain and lose heat by altering their behaviour, for example, many reptiles bask in the sun to warm up their bodies and move into the shade or water to cool down. Since reptiles do not use energy to regulate their body temperature, they can survive on much less food than similar-sized mammals. But it does mean that reptiles are restricted in where they can live and in colder regions they are inactive during the winter months.

CLASSIFICATION

About 2 million different organisms have been identified and sorted into groups, in a process called classification. Biologists look at the similarities and differences between organisms, and group together those with shared characteristics. The largest group is the kingdom, for example the animal kingdom. Each kingdom is divided into smaller groups, called phyla (singular: phylum). Each phylum is divided into classes, which are divided into orders, then families, genera and finally species. A species is a single type of organism with unique features that are different from all other organisms, for example a Nile crocodile. Only members of the same species can reproduce with each other and produce fertile offspring.

The classification of the Nile crocodile (*Crocodylus niloticus*) is shown on the right.

KINGDOM: Animalia
PHYLUM: Chordata
CLASS: Reptilia
ORDER: Crocodylia
FAMILY: Crocodylidae
GENUS: Crocodylus
SPECIES: *niloticus* (Nile crocodile)

One way of remembering the order of the different groups is to learn this phrase:
'**K**ings **P**lay **C**hess **O**n **F**ridays **G**enerally **S**peaking'.

Life cycle

Most reptiles lay eggs, which hatch into miniature versions of the adults. Reptilian eggs have a leathery shell, which protects the embryo inside and stops it from drying out. A few reptiles give birth to live young.

Classification

Reptiles are a class of vertebrates, along with fish, amphibians and mammals. The class is divided into four orders: turtles and tortoises; lizards and snakes; tuatara; and crocodiles and alligators. This book looks at the orders and some of the families within them, examining their characteristics and the way each group is adapted to its environment.

This young Florida red-bellied turtle (*Pseudemys nelsoni*) has just hatched from its egg. It is already recognizable as a turtle and will grow steadily throughout its life.

TURTLES AND TORTOISES (TESTUDINATA)

TURTLES AND TORTOISES ARE AN ANCIENT ORDER OF reptiles. They are found in most temperate and tropical regions, on land and in the sea. The order Testudinata contains just under 300 species, including tortoises, terrapins and turtles.

Shared features

Turtles and tortoises are the only vertebrates that have a bony shell. This unique feature is formed from the ribcage and part of the backbone. Turtles and tortoises have an unusual anatomy because their pectoral and pelvic girdles (their shoulders and hips) are positioned within their rib cage. Instead of teeth, they have a horny, toothless beak. They have five digits on each foot.

Shell armour

The shell is made up of two parts containing 50–60 bones. The upper, often domed part is called the carapace and it covers the back. The lower part, the plastron, covers the abdomen and front of the chest. The two parts of the shell are joined along the sides by a bony bridge. The shell

TORTOISE SKELETON

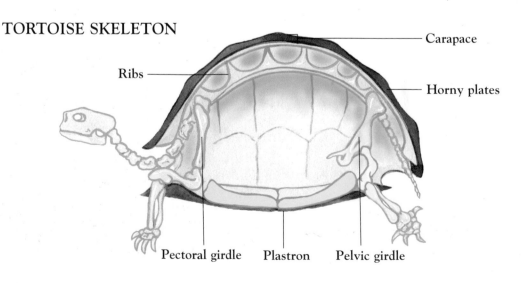

Carapace

Ribs

Horny plates

Pectoral girdle   Plastron   Pelvic girdle

offers protection from predators and often provides camouflage. Turtles and tortoises can withdraw their heads inside the shells. The dome-shaped shells are particularly difficult for predators to crush in their jaws. Not all carapaces are dome-shaped. Some tortoises have a relatively flat carapace so they can squeeze into rock crevices, while turtles are adapted to living in water by having flat, streamlined carapaces to help them swim.

This Hermann's tortoise (*Testudo hermanni*) is a straight-necked tortoise. When threatened, it can pull its head straight back inside its shell.

Classification

The order Testudinata is divided into two suborders: Peurodira (side-necked) and Cryptodira (straight-necked), according to how the tortoise or turtle draws its head into its shell. Straight-necked tortoises and turtles pull their heads straight back into the shell. Side-necked tortoises and turtles have longer necks, so they tuck their necks sideways into the shell's opening.

KEY CHARACTERISTICS
TESTUDINATA

- Bony shell made up of a carapace and plastron.
- Horny, toothless beak.
- Five digits on each foot.

What's the difference?

Tortoises are terrestrial animals and their shell is covered by horny scales. Their forelimbs are heavy with flattened, unwebbed toes. Turtles are mostly aquatic, although they do pull themselves out on to land. They tend to have a flatter shell and their toes are joined together by webbing. Their forelimbs are used like flippers or paddles for swimming.

Turtles, such as these green turtles (*Chelonia mydas*), swim long distances. Their flat shell slips easily through the water.

Living in water

Unlike most other reptiles, turtles spend much of their lives in and around water, and their bodies have adapted to their aquatic habitat. Turtles have lungs, not gills like fish, so they have to come to the surface to breathe. However, they have various adaptations to help them increase the time they can stay underwater, including being able to take in oxygen through the lining of their throat. Some turtles have a very slow metabolism, which means that they burn up food very slowly and do not need much oxygen. Loggerhead musk turtles can survive submerged underwater for hours or even days because their metabolism is so slow that they can absorb all the oxygen they need through their skin. These turtles can also survive in water that has low levels of oxygen, such as muddy channels. Turtles have flattened, paddle-like front limbs to help them swim.

Hawksbill turtles (*Eretmochelys imbricata*) live on coral reefs, where they feed on the coral, breaking off large chunks. They also eat sponges, seaweeds, jellyfish, crustaceans and small fish.

The alligator snapping turtle (*Macroclemys temminick*) has a small, red, worm-like projection at the end of its tongue (seen here), which it wiggles like bait to attract small fish.

Food and hunting

Most tortoises are herbivores. They feed on a range of plant foods such as leaves and fruits. Most turtles and terrapins are omnivores. They feed on a variety of plant and animal foods, such as corals, jellyfish, worms and molluscs. Since they are not fast-moving predators, they prey on slow-moving animals. Often they lie in wait for prey to pass close by, relying on camouflage to keep them hidden. When their prey comes into range, they strike. Some turtles and terrapins feed on tiny animals in the water using a sucking technique. They open their mouth and expand their throat at the same time, creating a vacuum that sucks in water and food.

Surviving the cold and heat

Like all reptiles, turtles and tortoises are able to survive extreme cold and heat by entering a state called aestivation, which is a bit like hibernation. Their body temperature falls even lower than normal and their metabolism slows considerably, so they can survive with very little oxygen or food. Desert tortoises and turtles aestivate during the hottest periods of the year. Tortoises and turtles that live in colder parts of the world survive the winters by creeping into holes or caves to aestivate. In Britain, owners of pet tortoises place them in cardboard boxes in a shed for the winter.

SPOTTED TURTLES

Spotted turtles of North America spend the winters sleeping in large groups of up to 23 individuals, on the bottoms of shallow rivers, ponds and lakes, often covered by ice. In the spring, the turtles emerge from the river and pond beds and spend much of the summer on land. In late October or early November, they return to the water again for the winter.

Turtle life cycle

Like most reptiles, turtles and tortoises lay eggs. They lay large clutches of up to 100 or more eggs, so that at least some will survive. The adults take no care of their eggs or the hatchlings. Most tortoises live between 40 and 60 years, some much longer.

Marine turtles live most of their life at sea, swimming across the oceans in search of food. When they are ready to breed, the adults swim back to traditional breeding beaches, a journey that can be thousands of kilometres. The turtles gather in the sea to mate. Then at high tide, when the sea reaches far up the beach, the females pull themselves on to the beach to lay their eggs. Each female digs a hole into which she lays about 100 eggs, before covering them with sand and leaving. The females may lay several clutches during the breeding season. The young turtles hatch between 50 and 60 days later, breaking out of the shell using an egg tooth on the tip of their beak before making a dash to the sea. The large number of turtle hatchlings that emerge together attracts predators such as lizards and birds, so only a few make it to the sea alive.

This female loggerhead turtle (*Caretta caretta*) has pulled herself to the top of the beach to lay her eggs. Most turtles come ashore under the cover of darkness to lay their eggs.

GALÁPAGOS GIANT TORTOISES

Galápagos giant tortoises (*Geochelone nigra*) live on the Galápagos islands, off the coast of Ecuador. These giant tortoises grow up to 1.3 m (4 ft) long and reach weights of up to 250 kg (550 lb). Many can live for more than 100 years. Galápagos giant tortoises do not mature (become ready to reproduce) until they are 20–25 years of age. Compared with most tortoises, the birth rate of Galápagos giant tortoises is extremely low because the females only lay 2–16 eggs in each clutch.

(Left) A female turtle digs a deep hole using her hind legs and quickly lays her eggs, before covering the nest with sand to protect the eggs from predators. The entire egg-laying process takes no more than three hours.

Tortoise life cycle

Most tortoises mate and lay their eggs in the spring. Some species lay their eggs in a hole dug in the ground, while others lay them under leaves. There are up to 100 eggs in a clutch. The young tortoises hatch between 60 and 120 days later, depending on the species.

Temperature and sex

Scientists have discovered that the sex of an unborn reptile in an egg can be influenced by the temperature of its surroundings. At the right temperature, approximately equal numbers of males and females hatch out, but if the temperature rises or falls slightly, there may be more of one sex. In turtles and tortoises, if the temperature falls slightly there are more males and if it rises by a couple of degrees, there are more females.

A Pacific pond turtle hatchling (*Clemmys marmorata*) breaks out of its shell. All the eggs in a turtle clutch hatch at the same time.

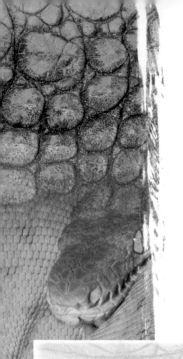

TUATARAS (RHYNCHOCEPHALIA)

TUATARAS ARE THE ONLY REMAINING RELATIVES OF A group of ancient reptiles that lived more than 200 million years ago. They survived when most of the dinosaurs died out, about 65 million years ago. Today tuataras are found only on 30 islands off the coast of New Zealand.

KEY CHARACTERISTICS
RHYNCHOCEPHALIA

- Two pairs of skull arches (a type of cheek bone under the eye).
- Abdominal ribs.
- Each rib has an uncinate process.
- Jawbones have serrated edges that form teeth.
- 'Third eye' connected to the brain.

Tuataras belong to the order Rhynchocephalia, which has just one family containing two species. The name 'tuatara' means 'old spiny back' in the Maori language, after the spiny necks and heads of these reptiles.

Shared features

Each of the tuatara's ribs has a small, bony projection at its back edge, called an uncinate process. This piece of bone forms a link between adjacent ribs, making the whole rib cage much stronger. The teeth of tuataras are unusual because they are part of the jawbone rather than separate structures. The teeth are not replaced when worn out or damaged, as they are in other reptiles such as crocodiles, so the oldest tuataras are virtually toothless, chewing their food between smooth jawbones. Another feature of tuataras is that, unlike other reptiles, they do not have an eardrum or a middle ear.

Tuataras have a 'third eye' on top of their head, which is connected to their brain. The third eye has a lens and a retina, but it is not actually involved with sight. It is, however, light-sensitive and scientists believe it may control the amount of time a tuatara spends basking in the sun. The third eye is visible only in hatchlings, when it has a translucent patch over the top. In adults, it is covered by their scaly skin.

Tuataras live in underground burrows, either digging their own or living in those made by burrowing seabirds. They are nocturnal (active at night) and feed on insects, earthworms and snails. They may also eat small lizards, amphibians and young seabirds.

Life cycle

Tuataras only reproduce once every three to four years. They usually mate in the summer (January in the southern hemisphere), but they do not lay eggs until the following summer. The female tuatara lays between 6 and 15 eggs in a nest and they take between 12 and 16 months to hatch.

ENDANGERED

Tuataras were once widespread in New Zealand, but today they are classed as endangered. In the mid-nineteenth century, they were hunted by people for food. Then rats arrived on settlers' ships from Europe. The rats ate the tuataras' eggs and killed their young. Today tuataras only live on a few islands that have rocky shores, making them inaccessible to people and their animals.

Tuataras are more active at lower temperatures than most other reptiles and their body temperature ranges from 6–13 °C, which is usually lower than their surroundings. The low temperatures at which they live mean that they grow slowly, so female tuataras are not mature and ready to breed until they are about 20 years old. Adults may live for more than 100 years.

Tuataras (*Sphenodon sp.*) are rather stout animals, with a thick tail. The adults grow up to 80 cm (30 in) long and weigh less than 1 kg (2.2 lb).

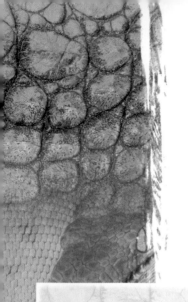

Snakes (Serpentes)

SNAKES ARE LEGLESS REPTILES. THEY ARE HIGHLY EFFICIENT, carnivorous predators, and one of the few groups of animals in which every member is a carnivore. Snakes are found worldwide apart from the polar regions, Iceland, Ireland, New Zealand and some of the smaller islands.

KEY CHARACTERISTICS
SERPENTES

- **Legless.**
- **No movable eyelids.**
- **No external ears.**
- **Large number of vertebrae in their backbone.**

Snakes belong to the order Squamata, along with lizards (see page 44). The snakes are placed in their own suborder, Serpentes. There are about 2,700 different species of snakes, including the adder, boa, python, cobra, grass snake and garter snake.

Snake features

The main feature of snakes is their lack of limbs. They also lack movable eyelids. Instead, snakes have transparent eyelids that are fused to form a special transparent scale, called the spectacle scale. Snakes lack external ears, but their sense of hearing is acute. Their ear bone is attached to their lower jaw and picks up vibrations as well as low-frequency noises. Their other senses, such as smell, are also well-developed. Some snakes have specialized sense organs not seen in other vertebrates, such as the heat-sensitive pits of the pitvipers (see page 23), and the Jacobson's organ in the roof of the mouth which is used for tasting. Snakes flick substances into the Jacobson's organ with their tongue.

Snakes, like this grass snake, moult (shed) their skin when it is worn out. Moulting also gets rid of parasites such as mites and ticks. During its moult, the snake usually hides and stops eating. It can be unusually aggressive at this time.

The shape of a snake's body is an adaptation to its lifestyle. Burrowing snakes tend to be shorter, with a stout body and short tail, while climbing snakes are generally longer and thinner. Most snakes have a single row of large, wide scales on their underside, which helps them to grip the ground. The scales covering the upper surface of the body tend to be smaller. Most snakes have more than 120 vertebrae in their backbone, but in some species there are as many as 585. Those with more vertebrae have stronger and more flexible spines. Snakes' internal organs have become elongated to fit into their long body. Paired organs such as the lungs and kidneys are arranged so that one lies above the other.

INTERNAL ORGANS

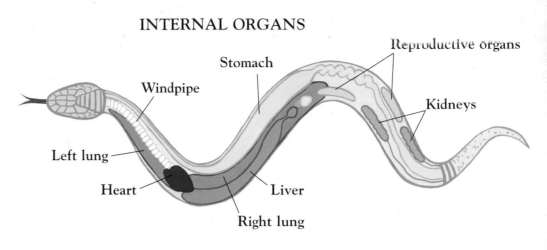

Reproductive organs

Stomach

Windpipe

Kidneys

Left lung

Heart

Liver

Right lung

Life cycle

Most female snakes lay leathery eggs in a nest. Most species give little parental care. The young snakes break out of the egg using an egg tooth. Once they have hatched, they slither into the undergrowth to escape predators.

Classification

The suborder Serpentes is divided into three groups called infraorders: blindsnakes, primitive snakes and advanced snakes. The three infraorders contain a total of 18 families. Five of these families are featured on pages 16–23: boas, pythons, colubrids, elapids and vipers.

Some snakes give birth to live young. The young develop in soft egg membranes inside the female's body. They break open the membrane soon after birth. This new-born smooth snake (*Coronella austriaca*) is still in its membrane.

BOAS AND PYTHONS (BOIDAE AND PYTHONIDAE)

BOAS AND PYTHONS ARE CONSTRICTING SNAKES THAT squeeze their prey to death. They include some of the largest snakes in the world. Both boas and pythons are found in Africa, Australia and Asia, while boas are also found in North and South America, and Madagascar.

Boas and pythons are two families in the primitive snakes infraorder. The boa family is made up of 28 species, including the boa constrictor and rubber boa, while the python family contains approximately 25 species, including the reticulated and rock python.

Shared features

Boas and pythons are characterized by a skull that is heavier than that of other snakes. Their jaw has an extra bone called the coronoid. Unusually, these snakes have a pelvic girdle (hips), which has been lost by other snakes through evolution. There are even remnants of back limbs, which appear as spurs. The spurs are more visible in male snakes, where they are seen near the tail. Unlike snakes in the advanced snakes infraorder (see pages 18–23), boas and pythons have two lungs, which are positioned one above the other in the body. Some boas and pythons have heat-sensitive pits in their jaws which help them to detect prey.

This Madagascar boa constrictor (*Acrantophis madagascariensis*) has caught and wrapped its body around a lizard. The lizard will be swallowed head first.

Killing prey

Boas and pythons kill by coiling their heavy body around the prey animal and squeezing, for example pythons will kill deer. The coils get tighter as the prey animal struggles. Once the animal has been suffocated, the snake relaxes the coils and starts to eat the animal whole, head first. Its lower jaw can dislocate and swing open in order to swallow large prey. The jaws on either side work alternately, slowly 'walking' the body into the mouth. Once swallowed, the prey animal is slowly digested.

Getting around

Tree boas can move remarkably quickly from tree to tree. Their long body is adapted for living in trees by having a prehensile tail that can wrap around branches. Tree boas move by extending their head and the upper part of their body out from one branch to another, gripping firmly with their long prehensile tail. Most tree boas rest coiled up around a branch with their head hanging down, ready to catch any passing prey.

The tree boa (*Corallus enydris*) is a nocturnal snake found in the rainforests of Central and South America.

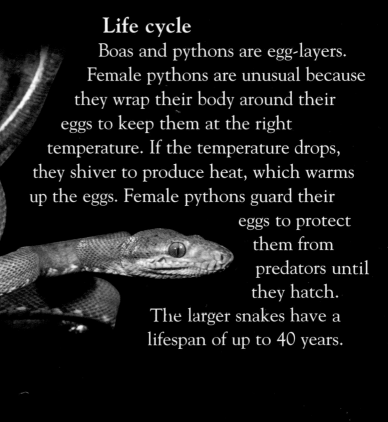

Life cycle

Boas and pythons are egg-layers. Female pythons are unusual because they wrap their body around their eggs to keep them at the right temperature. If the temperature drops, they shiver to produce heat, which warms up the eggs. Female pythons guard their eggs to protect them from predators until they hatch. The larger snakes have a lifespan of up to 40 years.

COLUBRIDS (COLUBRIDAE)

THE FAMILY COLUBRIDAE BELONGS TO THE INFRAORDER of advanced snakes. This is a huge and varied family of about 1,600 species, including the garter, grass, corn, snail-eating, kingsnake and milk snake. They are found worldwide except in the polar regions and the northernmost parts of North America and Asia.

Shared features

All colubrids lack a functioning left lung. Unlike the boas and pythons, colubrids do not have a pelvic girdle or any remnants of hind limbs, nor do they have a coronoid bone in their jaw. However, colubrids tend to have a jaw that is even more flexible than the constrictors because the upper and lower jaws are not connected to each other. Most colubrids have a distinct head and tapering body. The burrowing species are exceptions – they are streamlined, with no distinct neck between the head and the shortish body. Most colubrids have large, plate-like scales on their head.

This grass snake (*Natrix natrix*) has opened its jaws wide in order to swallow a toad. The toad has inflated its body to make it look bigger than it really is and to make it more difficult for it to be swallowed.

Hunting

Colubrids use a variety of hunting and killing methods. Many are fast-moving diurnal (day) hunters but there are nocturnal species, too, such as the mangrove snake and kingsnake. Some species constrict their prey, while others use venom (poison). Colubrids have solid fangs, so their venom travels along a groove on the surface of the fang into their wounded prey.

Garter snakes are diurnal. They hunt during the day making good use of their sight, hearing (sensing ground vibrations), taste and smell. They are quite agile and can cover the ground quickly. In contrast, the mangrove snake rarely leaves the trees. It is a nocturnal snake that moves through the trees with grace and speed. When not hunting, the mangrove snake curls up and spends the day motionless.

Surviving the cold

Snakes cannot cope with the cold climate of northern latitudes so they survive by sheltering underground and aestivating through the winter. For example, the garter snakes of North America crawl into large holes and caves where they pile up together to reduce heat loss. When the temperatures rise again in spring, they emerge together.

KEY CHARACTERISTICS
COLUBRIDAE

- No functioning left lung.
- No pelvic spurs visible and no remnants of pelvic girdle.
- No coronoid bone in jaw.

The mangrove snake (*Boiga dendrophila*) is a nocturnal predator that relies on its sense of hearing and smell to find prey.

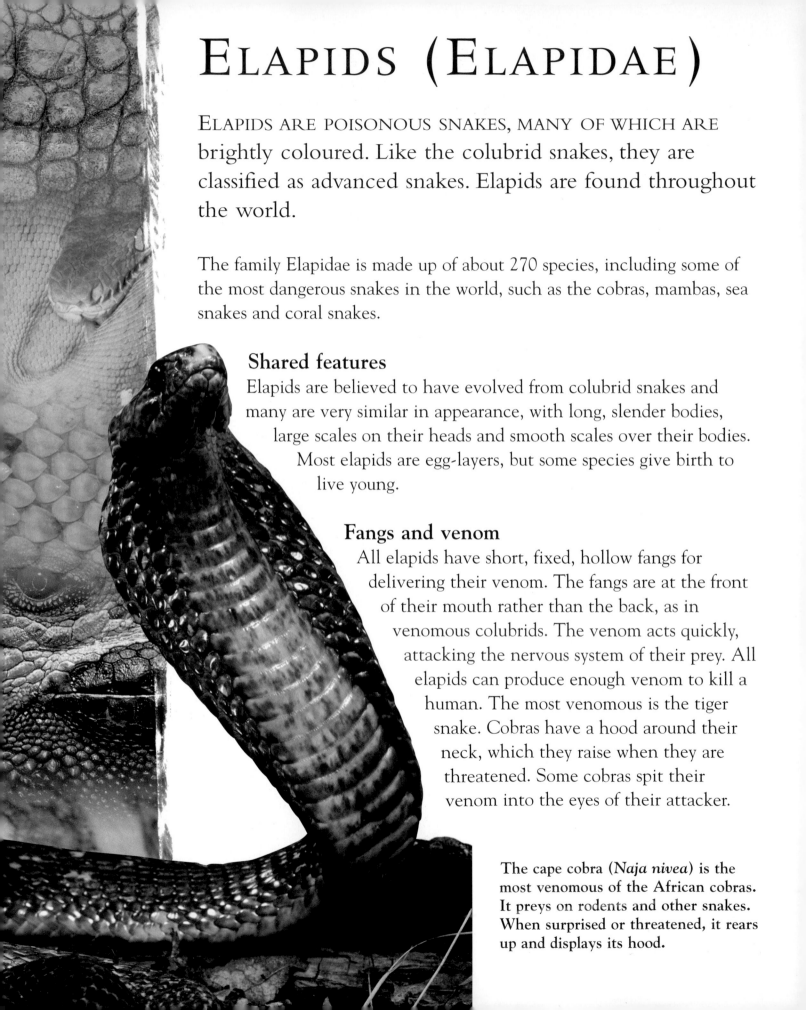

ELAPIDS (ELAPIDAE)

ELAPIDS ARE POISONOUS SNAKES, MANY OF WHICH ARE brightly coloured. Like the colubrid snakes, they are classified as advanced snakes. Elapids are found throughout the world.

The family Elapidae is made up of about 270 species, including some of the most dangerous snakes in the world, such as the cobras, mambas, sea snakes and coral snakes.

Shared features

Elapids are believed to have evolved from colubrid snakes and many are very similar in appearance, with long, slender bodies, large scales on their heads and smooth scales over their bodies. Most elapids are egg-layers, but some species give birth to live young.

Fangs and venom

All elapids have short, fixed, hollow fangs for delivering their venom. The fangs are at the front of their mouth rather than the back, as in venomous colubrids. The venom acts quickly, attacking the nervous system of their prey. All elapids can produce enough venom to kill a human. The most venomous is the tiger snake. Cobras have a hood around their neck, which they raise when they are threatened. Some cobras spit their venom into the eyes of their attacker.

The cape cobra (*Naja nivea*) is the most venomous of the African cobras. It preys on rodents and other snakes. When surprised or threatened, it rears up and displays its hood.

Most elapids have colours that provide good camouflage, such as shades of green and brown, but the coral snakes have red and black warning colours. Coral snakes are small snakes that spend much of their time underground, feeding primarily on other snakes. They may be small, but their venom is very poisonous.

Living in water

Most elapids are terrestrial (live on land), but a number are arboreal (live in trees) and some burrow in the ground. Sea kraits and sea snakes are aquatic, and adapted to life in the sea. They have flattened tails that they use for swimming. Sea snakes have nostrils that they can close when underwater. They give birth to live young while at sea. Sea kraits live in the sea but they have to come ashore to lay their eggs. Both sea snakes and sea kraits feed mainly on fish, which they kill and eat quickly so the fish do not sink to the sea floor.

Sea kraits such as this one (*Laticauda sp.*) are excellent swimmers. Since they breathe air, they have to close their nostrils when they dive so they do not get a nose full of water.

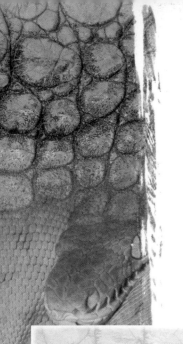

VIPERS (VIPERIDAE)

VIPERS ARE A FAMILY OF POISONOUS SNAKES, CONSIDERED to be the most highly evolved of all the snakes. They belong to the advanced snakes (Caeophidia). There are about 230 species, including the pitviper, adder, Gabon viper and sidewinder. They are found further north and south in the world than other snakes.

KEY CHARACTERISTICS
VIPERIDAE
- **Long, hollow fangs.**
- **Triangular-shaped head.**
- **Give birth to live young.**

Shared features

Vipers have long, hollow fangs that can be folded against the roof of the mouth when not in use. Their bodies range in length from about 25 cm (10 in) to just under 4 m (13 ft). Their heads have a distinctive, triangular shape, which is due in part to the presence of the fangs and the muscles of the venom glands. Vipers have rough scales. Their heads are covered with lots of small scales and their eyes have vertical pupils. They are often camouflaged. Most give birth to live young.

The poison of vipers works differently from that of the elapids. It attacks the tissues and blood. The Russell's viper is responsible for more human deaths than any other snake because it has such a wide distribution, from Pakistan across Southeast Asia.

Gabon vipers (*Bitis gabonica*) have the longest fangs of any snake, measuring up to 4 cm (1.5 in) long. The colour of these snakes provides good camouflage among dead leaves on the ground.

Sidewinders

Most snakes move across the ground by throwing their body into a series of curves and pushing against the ground. Others glide forwards in a straight line. Sidewinders have a unique method of moving that is an adaptation to having to cross sand in hot deserts. They move sideways, with only a couple of parts of their body in contact with the ground at any one time. This prevents the snake's abdomen from resting on the hot sand for too long. Sidewinding snakes leave an S-shaped trail in the sand.

Pitvipers

Pitvipers have a pair of heat-sensing pits between their eyes and their nostrils, which allow them to hunt at night. The heat-detecting sensors detect temperature differences between objects and their surroundings, so they are ideal for hunting mammals and birds at night. Some pitvipers also use their sensors to find cool places to shelter from high daytime temperatures.

Rattlesnakes

Rattlesnakes have a rattle at the end of their tail which they shake when threatened to scare off predators. The rattle is made up of dried scales. It is built up every time the snake sheds its skin, leaving an enlarged scale at the end of its tail.

(Above) Rattlesnakes such as this Arizona black rattlesnake (*Crotalus viridis cerberus*) shake their rattle to warn animals to stay away. It is thought that rattlesnakes developed their rattle because it made a louder noise than the sound of their tail shaken against dry vegetation.

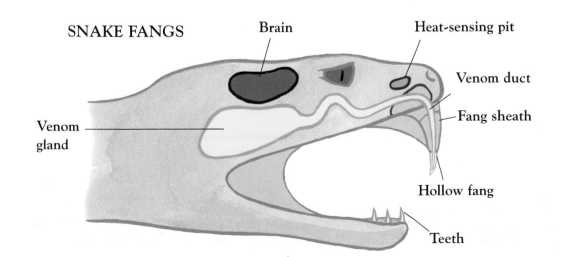

SNAKE FANGS

Brain

Heat-sensing pit

Venom duct

Fang sheath

Venom gland

Hollow fang

Teeth

(Left) The delivery of venom is a bit like a hypodermic needle. When the fangs bite, the muscles on the venom gland are squeezed, which forces the venom through the duct in the fang and out into the wound.

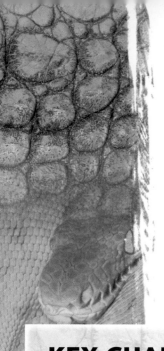

LIZARDS (LACERTILIA)

LIZARDS ARE A LARGE, SUCCESSFUL GROUP OF REPTILES. They are found around the world as far north as Canada and as far south as the tip of South America.

Lizards belong to the same order as snakes – Squamata. Within Squamata they form the suborder Lacertilia. There are about 4,500 species of lizards, including geckos, monitors, skinks, chameleons and iguanas.

KEY CHARACTERISTICS
LACERTILIA

- Most have a 'fragile' tail.
- External ear opening.
- Movable eyelids.
- Long tongue.
- 'Third eye' connected to the brain.

Shared features

The most obvious difference between lizards and snakes is that most lizards have four limbs. They hold their limbs out at right angles to their bodies, so that when they walk, their bodies sway from side to side with their long tail swinging behind. Lizards have small, sharp teeth along the edges of their jaws. Their teeth fall out and are replaced frequently. Lizards have an external ear opening and eyelids that

This Jackson's chameleon (*Chamaeleo jacksonii*) belongs to the suborder Iguania, which includes chameleons and iguanas. Jackson's chameleon has a particularly thick, scaly skin.

can open and close. Their tongue is long and can be extended beyond their mouth to catch prey. Like tuataras, lizards have a light-sensitive area at the top of their head called the 'third eye', which is connected to the brain (see page 12).

Losing their tail

Many lizards can voluntarily shed their tail when threatened or caught by a predator. This is called autotomy and it allows the lizard to escape while the predator watches the tail thrash around on the floor. Lizards can shed their tails because most have a 'fragile' tail – a tail with a weak joint between two vertebrae. After it has been shed, the tail regrows.

Scales

The lizard's scaly skin is generally thick and very tough, giving valuable protection. The size and shape of lizard scales vary. In many species, the scales are generally large and often rough to the touch. In others, the scales are small and very smooth. Mostly, the scales overlap but in some species, the scales just touch each other. In some species, such as iguanas, the scales are modified to form spines, while in others, such as the Namib plated lizard, they are strengthened by bony plates.

This Komodo dragon (*Varanus komodoensis*) hatchling is breaking out of its shell. The Komodo dragon female lays about 20–25 eggs, each of which is twice the size of a chicken egg. The eggs hatch after about nine months.

Life cycle

Most lizards lay eggs, although the females of a few species retain the eggs within their body and give birth to live young. The young are well-developed.

The suborder Lacertilia is divided into four superfamilies: iguanas and chameleons; geckos; skinks and wall lizards; and monitors.

IGUANAS AND CHAMELEONS (IGUANIA)

IGUANAS AND CHAMELEONS MAKE UP A LARGE superfamily that is divided into three families: iguanas, agamids, and chameleons. They are a diverse group of lizards that vary in shape, size and colour.

Physical features

One of the main differences between iguanas, agamas and chameleons is their teeth. Most iguanas have teeth that are attached to sockets on the inside of their jaw. These teeth are not replaced when lost. Agamids and chameleons both have acrodont teeth, where the teeth are not in sockets but firmly attached to the jawbone.

Iguanas

There are about 700 species of iguanas found in North and South America, and some islands such as Madagascar and the Fiji islands. They have well-developed limbs and a fragile tail. Most are terrestrial (land-living) or arboreal (tree-dwelling), but some live near the sea. The marine iguanas of the Galápagos Islands have webbed feet and a flattened tail. They live on the coast, where they feed on algae in the water. Other iguanas live in deserts and one of their adaptations is the ability to become a lighter colour during the day to reflect heat. Some iguanas develop bright colours during the breeding season, such as a bright-red or blue throat and abdomen.

The thorny devil (*Moloch horridus*) is a type of agamid that is found in the Australian desert. It is covered in protective, spiny lumps. Tiny channels between its scales direct dew or rain towards its mouth.

Agamids or chisel-teeth lizards

Agamids are found in Africa and across Asia to Australia. There are about 420 different species. Most have a large head with a thick, fleshy tongue, a cylindrical body and a fragile tail.

CHAMELEON COLOUR

Chameleons can change the colour of their body to help them hide from predators. They change colour in response to changes in the light, background, temperature, or simply their mood. Chameleons have pigment-containing cells called chromatophores in their skin. They change colour when their brain sends a message to the cells, causing them to get larger or shrink, and this changes the colour of their skin.

These lizards are diurnal (active during the day). They hunt for small animals such as insects. Many male agamids have breeding colours to attract females and they will bob their head up and down in front of the female during courtship.

Chameleons

Chameleons are found across Africa, in southern Europe, and across Asia to India and Sri Lanka. They have a long, generally narrow, flattened body. Their head is pointed, with large eyes that can move independently. Instead of a fragile tail, chameleons have a prehensile tail that can wrap around branches. Chameleons are arboreal and adapted to life in trees. They move slowly along branches, gripping firmly with their long toes and tail. This slow movement makes a chameleon difficult to spot, especially when its skin colour matches its surroundings.

This Jackson's chameleon (*Chamaeleo jacksonii*) has caught a grasshopper with its long, sticky tongue. Researchers have calculated that a chameleon's tongue shoots out at speeds of more than 26 body lengths per second – that's the equivalent of 22 km/h (13 mph). Chameleons can catch prey up to 1.5 body lengths away.

Geckos (Gekkota)

GECKOS ARE NOCTURNAL LIZARDS THAT ARE WELL known for their calls and their ability to run up walls. They are found in North and South America, Africa, Asia and Australia.

The superfamily Gekkota contains more than 930 species divided into four families: eyelid geckos, geckos, Southwest Pacific geckos, and flap-footed lizards.

Shared features

Geckos are small, slender lizards, with a large, flat head. Their eyes are relatively large and, as in snakes, are protected by a spectacle scale. Geckos do not have eyelids, so they use their long tongue to wipe dirt off the surface of the eye. Their bodies are covered in soft scales.

Running up walls

Climbing geckos have specialized feet that allow them to run up walls and across ceilings. Their toes have enlarged pads with overlapping scales underneath. Each of these scales bears thousands of tiny hairs. The hairs form a temporary bond with the surface on which the gecko is walking, which is broken when the foot is lifted.

A gecko's foot is covered in millions of minuscule hairs, called setae, with tiny pads at their tips. The feet do not pick up dirt because any particles of dirt are repelled by the setae.

When threatened, the leaf-tail gecko (*Uroplatus fimbriatus*) lifts its tail and opens its mouth wide to display its bright-red tongue.

KEY CHARACTERISTICS
GEKKOTA

- **Vertical pupils.**
- **Hairs on toes for gripping.**
- **Spectacle scales.**

Behaviour

Most geckos are nocturnal, but there are some diurnal geckos. Nocturnal geckos feed on a range of small animals, from insects and spiders to small snakes, birds and even mammals. Diurnal geckos eat fruit and pollen, too. All geckos find their prey using sight and smell.

Geckos are very noisy lizards. They make a range of sounds from their well-developed larynx (voice box), including chirps, clicks and growls. Male geckos are territorial and make sounds to warn off other males.

Life cycle

Most geckos lay only one or two eggs. The eggs usually have hard shells, although a few species lay eggs with soft shells. The young use a special egg tooth on the top of their nose to break out of the egg. A few species of geckos give birth to live young.

SKINKS (SCINCIDAE)

THESE SMALL LIZARDS BELONG TO THE SUPERFAMILY Scinomorpha, together with wall and sand lizards. The family contains more than 1,400 species, found in a wide variety of habitats worldwide except the northern regions of Russia, Canada, Alaska and Antarctica.

Shared features

Most skinks have a cylindrical body and short legs. They range in size from a few centimetres to 50 cm (20 in) long. Their scales are generally smooth and overlap each other. Most have a relatively small, wedge-shaped head. A few species, such as blind burrowing skinks, have either very small limbs or no limbs at all. Blind burrowing skinks spend their lives underground feeding on insects. Their bodies are covered in small scales and they move by 'swimming' through the soil or sand.

Most skinks are diurnal (active during the day) and insectivorous, feeding on a range of insects. Some are omnivores, for example, the blue-tongued skink feeds on fruits, flowers, snails, and birds' eggs as well as insects. The Solomon Islands skink is unusual because it is herbivorous, feeding solely on plant material.

When threatened, the northern blue-tongued skink (*Tiliqua scincoides intermedia*) opens its mouth to show off its blue tongue. If the threat does not go away, the skink may hiss and flatten its body, making itself look bigger.

Egg laying

Most skinks lay eggs. Some lay just a single egg, whereas others lay clutches of 30 or more. Most species lay their eggs and leave them, but a few species, such as five-lined skinks, look after their eggs. They turn them regularly to move the embryo inside and prevent it sticking to one side.

The female broad-headed skink (*Eumeces laticeps*) lays 6–16 eggs between May and July, under logs or in leaf litter. The eggs hatch after about a month.

A few species, such as the Solomon Islands skink, give birth to live young. Some, such as the Brazilian skink, show a unique feature. Female Brazilian skinks retain tiny eggs inside their bodies. The eggs lack a yolk, so the embryo gets its food directly from its mother via a placenta-like structure – a method that is very similar to mammals. The gestation period is almost a year.

Some skinks are long-lived, for example, the shingleback can live for up to 20 years. Male and female shinglebacks form pairs that stay together for many years. The pairs separate after mating, but they find each other again at the beginning of each breeding season.

KEY CHARACTERISTICS
SCINCIDAE

- Small, wedge-shaped heads.
- Generally smooth, overlapping scales.
- Cylindrical body with a long, 'fragile' tail.
- Round pupils.

WALL AND SAND LIZARDS (LACERTIDAE)

WALL AND SAND LIZARDS BELONG TO THE FAMILY Lacertidae. They are closely related to skinks and belong to the same superfamily – Scinomorpha. There are about 200 species, found across Africa, Europe and much of Asia.

Shared features

Wall and sand lizards are relatively small, up to about 25 cm (10 in) in length. Most have a conical-shaped head, with a pointed snout and a fold of skin across the throat. Their feet have long digits, which are suited to running over sand or climbing. Their bodies are covered by small scales on the upper surface and by large, rectangular scales on the lower surface. Their tail is particularly long and fragile. Unlike the skinks, wall and sand lizards have eyes with movable eyelids. The tongue is long and narrow, with a deep fork at the tip.

Wall and sand lizards are mostly terrestrial. They are active during the day, feeding on invertebrate animals such as insects. They will also tackle small lizards, snakes and even small mammals.

During early spring and late autumn, the viviparous, or common lizard (*Lacerta vivipara*) spends a lot of time basking in the sun. When the lizard emerges in the morning its body temperature is about 15 °C (59 °F). It needs to warm up to about 30 °C (86 °F) to become active. It does not bask as much in summer because the temperatures are warmer.

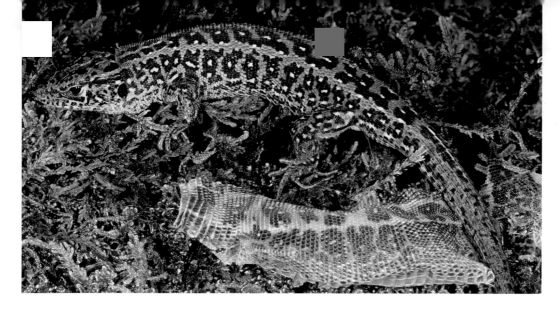

This male sand lizard (*Lacerta agilis*) has just shed its skin. During the breeding season, the males have bright-green sides. The female lays eggs in burrows dug in the sand.

Life cycle

Most wall and sand lizards lay eggs. The viviparous lizard, which is found as far north as the Arctic Circle, is the only lizard to give birth to live young. Egg-layers cannot survive so far north because it is too cold for their eggs to be incubated. Viviparous lizards avoid this problem by keeping their eggs inside their bodies and giving birth to up to 11 live young at a time.

Male sand lizards develop breeding colours and perform courtship displays to attract females. The males often fight over females, threatening each other at first by moving their head up and down. Sometimes they also flatten their bodies to look larger. Sand lizards also use simple sounds such as clicks to attract females and defend their territory.

KEY CHARACTERISTICS
LACERTIDAE

- Small, conical head with a pointed snout.
- Feet with long digits.
- Fold of skin across the throat.
- Long 'fragile' tail.

Surviving in deserts

Many wall and sand lizards are found in dry habitats, such as deserts and heathland, where they have adapted to the lack of water. Desert-dwelling lizards have fringes at the ends of their toes to help them run on the sand. The shovel-snouted lizard of the Namib Desert feeds on the surface of sand dunes. When threatened by predators, or to escape the high daytime temperatures, it buries itself in the sand. While hunting, this lizard is often seen with two of its legs raised to avoid the hot sand and to allow cooler air to circulate around its body.

MONITORS (ANGUIMORPHA)

MONITORS INCLUDE SOME OF THE LARGEST LIZARDS, SUCH as the impressive Komodo dragon and the only poisonous lizard, the Gila monster. These lizards are found mostly in the tropics, as well as throughout Europe, the Middle East and parts of central South and North America, living in a variety of habitats from deserts to tropical rainforests.

Anguimorpha is a large superfamily of 175 species divided into five families: anguids, xenosaurs, beaded lizards, Bornean earless monitors, and monitor lizards.

Shared features

Monitors have rectangular scales covering their bodies and some have skin folds along their sides. Most have four legs but a few, such as the slow-worm, are legless. All monitors have movable eyelids and all but the Bornean earless monitors have external ear openings. Most species, particularly the slow-worm, have fragile tails that come off readily.

Anguids

Anguid lizards are found in deserts, grasslands and forests. Some are active during the day, but others are nocturnal. Alligator lizards are found in tropical rainforests, high up in the canopy. They have a long, prehensile

The slow-worm (*Anguis fragilis*) may look like a snake, but it is actually a legless lizard that belongs to the anguid family. It is often called the blind worm after its tiny eyes, although it can see.

The Komodo dragon (*Varanus komodoensis*) is the largest lizard in the world. When attacking large prey such as goats, this lizard attacks the feet and lower legs with its teeth, inflicting terrible bites as it tries to pull the animal down.

KEY CHARACTERISTICS
ANGUIMORPHA

- Rectangular scales.
- Movable eyelids.
- External ear openings.
- Most have a 'fragile' tail.

tail that wraps itself around branches to provide a firm grip. Alligator lizards are often brightly coloured. The California legless lizards are burrowing lizards found in sandy soils. Able to detect their prey from vibrations, they quickly come to the surface, grab the prey and disappear again.

Monitor lizards

Monitor lizards tend to have a long neck and a narrow head, a long, forked tongue and a muscular tail that is not fragile, so it cannot be detached. The largest monitor lizard is the Komodo dragon, which grows up to 3 m (10 ft) long including the tail. The Komodo dragon has wide jaws, a fold of skin on its neck and incredibly long, sharp claws. It uses its long, muscular tail as a prop when standing on its hind legs. It also uses it as a weapon. The Komodo dragon uses its good sense of smell to find both live prey and the decaying remains of animals. Its saliva contains harmful bacteria, which can infect the bites it makes on its prey, often leading to death.

CROCODILIANS (CROCODYLIA)

CROCODILIANS ARE THE LARGEST LIVING REPTILES. They are an ancient order of reptiles that are more closely related to the dinosaurs than other reptiles. One of the reasons that they have survived for millions of years is because they are highly successful predators.

The order Crocodylia contains 23 species, which are divided between three families: alligators, crocodiles, and gharials. Crocodilians range in size from Cuvier's dwarf caiman, which grows to about 1.5 m (5 ft) long, to the Indopacific crocodile, which grows to a massive 7 m (23 ft) long.

Shared features

All crocodilians have a similar body shape – wide and flattened, with the head held out in front and the legs held out to the sides. Their flattened, muscular tails are an efficient shape for swimming. Most have a long snout, with nostrils positioned on top of their head so that they lie just above the water's surface while the rest of the body is submerged. Crocodilians have a third eyelid, called a nictitating membrane, which is transparent and protects the eye when the crocodile is diving. Their scales are large and bony with raised ridges, giving excellent protection. Crocodilians shed their scales one at a time rather than moulting like snakes. In their mouth, they have a flap of skin, called a false palate, which closes off the trachea (tube to the lungs) so they can feed underwater without risk of drowning. Their ears are covered by flaps, which close to prevent water from entering.

Morelet's crocodile (*Crocodylus moreletii*) is one of the smaller crocodile species, reaching about 3 m (10 ft) in length. It is found in Central America.

All three types of crocodilian have adapted to a semi-aquatic life, living in and near water. Some have even moved into salt water. However, all crocodilians must lay their eggs on land.

Alligators

The alligator family includes alligators and caimans. They all live in North and South America, apart from the Chinese alligator, which lives in eastern China. Their snout is broad and blunt, and the teeth on their lower jaw lie inside their mouth so their teeth are not visible when their mouth is closed.

The long, thin snout with its bulbous tip is one of the main characteristics of gharials, such as this male Indian gharial (*Gavialis gangeticus*). The gharial's name comes from the Indian word 'ghara', which means 'rounded pot'.

Crocodiles

Crocodiles live mainly in Asia and Africa, but some are found in Florida, the Caribbean, and Central and South America. Some species have long, slender snouts, whereas in others the snout is broad and short. The fourth tooth on the lower jaw of crocodiles is exposed when their mouths are closed.

Gharials

Gharials are found in India, Nepal, Pakistan and Bangladesh. Their body looks just like an alligator, but their snout is very different. It is elongated and flattened, and in males, it ends with a bulbous tip. The shape of their snout makes it easier for gharials to catch fish. They swing their head from side to side so that the snout acts like a trap, catching many fish at once.

KEY CHARACTERISTICS
CROCODYLIA

- Head held out horizontally in front of the body.
- Snout with nostrils lying on top.
- Large, bony scales.
- Muscular, flattened tail.

The female Nile crocodile (*Crocodylus niloticus*) lays 25–100 eggs, which she covers with sand. The young crocodiles hatch three months later.

Life cycle

All crocodilians are egg-layers. The females lay their eggs on land, in nests made from plant material or mud. The adults, especially the females, stay close to the nest to guard the eggs from predators such as monitor lizards and baboons. All the eggs in the nest hatch at the same time. Often, the hatchlings need help to leave the nest, for example, if the mud has dried very hard. The parent crocodiles give considerable care to their hatchlings, with both adults often staying close to them for several weeks or even months after they hatch. The adults respond quickly to their hatchlings' cries of distress. Saltwater crocodiles are particularly aggressive in the defence of their eggs and hatchlings.

Getting older

Crocodilians become sexually mature (able to mate) once they reach a certain age and size. Their size is just as important as their age because a crocodile that is not large enough will not be able to mate, even if it is old enough. Like turtles, a crocodilian's sex is determined by the temperature of the environment during the development of the egg (see page 11). Crocodilians continue to grow throughout their entire lives, even after they have reached sexual maturity.

Territories

Adult male crocodilians are territorial and they mark their territory by loudly slapping their heads or snapping their jaws on the surface of the water. The larger, older males are often the dominant animals. They have the largest territories with the best nesting sites and places to bask. The territories of some males may include the nesting sites of several females. Fights between crocodilians are rare, but they sometimes take place between males of the same size who are competing for dominance. When two male crocodilians fight, they line up next to each other facing opposite directions and bang the sides of their heads together.

Nile crocodiles (*Crocodylus niloticus*) take great care of their eggs. This adult is helping a young crocodile to hatch by gently cracking the shell of the egg.

SOUNDS

Crocodilians make a range of sounds. The hatchlings call to the adults when they are in danger, and they are also very vocal while being fed. The sounds produced by the hatchlings or adults help to keep the hatchlings together. Adult crocodilians also communicate with other adults. The most common adult sound is a loud, low roar, which is repeated and may be echoed by other adults as a way of communicating.

Hunting

Crocodilians are some of the world's most fearsome predators. Most hunt by lying concealed underwater and waiting for prey to come close. Crocodilians are capable of short bursts of high speed to catch their prey, but they cannot keep up the chase for long, so they have to surprise their prey. Some crocodilians drift slowly in the water, with only the tips of their eyes showing. Caimans use their long tail to trap fish in shallow water. Crocodilians are normally solitary animals, but when there is a lot of food available they sometimes gather and even hunt together. This happens during the annual migration of wildebeest in Africa, when thousands of animals cross the River Mara in Kenya.

Crocodile food

Crocodilians are opportunistic hunters and they eat whatever they can catch. Most eat insects, tadpoles, frogs, snails, crabs, shrimps, birds and small fish. They also eat snakes, turtles and bats. The larger species, such as the Nile and saltwater crocodiles, will tackle mammals, while the caiman will attack anacondas. All crocodilians have strong jaw muscles for biting and holding their prey. Usually the prey animal is drowned and then swallowed, head first, either whole or in chunks.

Each year during their annual migration, thousands of wildebeest have to cross the Mara River, in Kenya. Nile crocodiles (*Crocodylus niloticus*) lie in wait in the water and grab animals as they swim across.

Storing fat

Crocodilians convert more than half the food they eat into fat, which is stored in their tail and back. These fat stores are used during times when the animals cannot find prey. A study of Nile crocodiles indicated that they eat only about 50 meals a year, yet they are able to survive for long periods without any food. Some of the larger crocodilians may be able to survive up to two years between meals.

DIGESTION

The crocodilian stomach is the most acidic of any vertebrate. This means that crocodiles can digest more than most predators, including the bones and shells of prey animals. Their digestion is aided by a muscular gizzard in their stomach, which is a sac containing stones that helps to break down food.

Keeping cool

Crocodilians bask in the sun during the day to raise their body temperature, returning to the water to cool off. They can also cool off by opening their mouths, which exposes a large surface from which water can evaporate. Often, crocodilians avoid the hot sun by remaining underwater or in mud during the day. However, many crocodiles tend to lie in the sun after eating because the heat helps to speed up digestion.

Caimans are found in South America. This spectacled caiman (*Caiman crocodilus*) has a piranha fish in its jaws. 'Caiman' is a Spanish word that means 'alligator'.

UNDER THREAT

REPTILE SPECIES ARE UNDER THREAT ALL OVER THE WORLD. Among the many reasons are habitat loss, poaching, water pollution and global warming.

Habitat loss

Many turtle habitats are being destroyed by tourism. Turtles return to traditional breeding beaches to lay their eggs. Often, these are the same beaches used by tourists, who stay in hotels that have been built nearby. The disturbance from the tourists and from the hotel lights prevents the turtles from laying their eggs, which means their numbers decline. Turtles are also threatened because in many parts of the world their eggs are collected and eaten as a delicacy.

Terrestrial reptiles, especially snakes and lizards that live in tropical rainforests, are also losing their habitats. Rainforests are being cleared at an ever-increasing rate to make room for farming and new houses. Habitats are being polluted, too. The seas and rivers where reptiles live are being polluted by sewage, oil and other chemicals. As the human population grows, people are moving into new areas and coming into contact with snakes, particularly in India. Often, snakes are killed because they are poisonous and could harm people.

Snake skin is used to make a wide range of clothes, shoes and bags. Some skins come from legally farmed snakes, but there is a thriving illegal trade and this is endangering the survival of some snake species in the wild.

Killed for their skin

Many reptiles are hunted for their skins, including sea kraits, alligators, crocodiles and caimans. Their skins are used to make goods such as handbags, briefcases and shoes. This has led to a drastic fall in the numbers of some species.

These reseachers are removing the eggs from the nest of a loggerhead turtle (*Caretta caretta*), on a beach in Queensland, Australia. The eggs will be incubated and the hatchlings released. This way more hatchlings will survive.

Saving reptiles

Not all reptiles are declining in number. The number of saltwater crocodiles in northern Australia has risen to more than 75,000 from almost nothing due to the introduction of hunting controls in 1971. Many turtle breeding beaches, for example in Australia, Malaysia and Indonesia, are now being protected. Often the eggs are removed and hatched in captivity to increase the number of hatchlings being released into the sea. By carefully controlling the temperature at which the eggs develop, it is possible to produce more female turtles, which will help boost the numbers in the future.

SNAKE SKIN

Sea kraits (see page 21) have been wiped out in the seas around many small, tropical islands because they are easy to catch and their skin makes high-quality leather. Scientists believe that if the numbers of sea kraits killed were controlled more carefully, it would be possible to maintain their numbers and still allow some hunting to take place.

REPTILE CLASSIFICATION

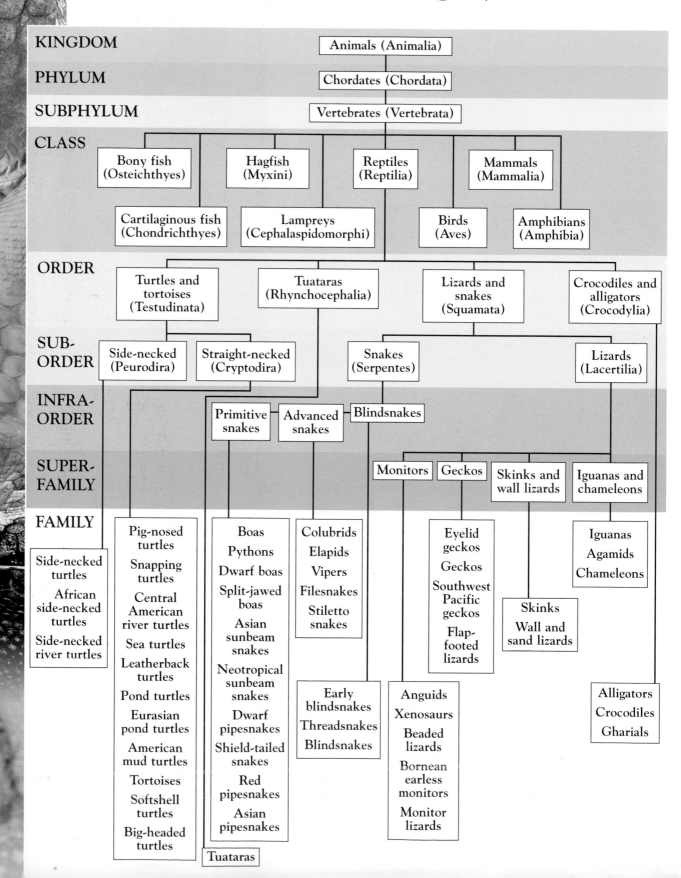

KINGDOM	Animals (Animalia)
PHYLUM	Chordates (Chordata)
SUBPHYLUM	Vertebrates (Vertebrata)

CLASS

- Bony fish (Osteichthyes)
- Hagfish (Myxini)
- Reptiles (Reptilia)
- Mammals (Mammalia)
- Cartilaginous fish (Chondrichthyes)
- Lampreys (Cephalaspidomorphi)
- Birds (Aves)
- Amphibians (Amphibia)

ORDER

- Turtles and tortoises (Testudinata)
- Tuataras (Rhynchocephalia)
- Lizards and snakes (Squamata)
- Crocodiles and alligators (Crocodylia)

SUB-ORDER

- Side-necked (Peurodira)
- Straight-necked (Cryptodira)
- Snakes (Serpentes)
- Lizards (Lacertilia)

INFRA-ORDER

- Primitive snakes
- Advanced snakes
- Blindsnakes

SUPER-FAMILY

- Monitors
- Geckos
- Skinks and wall lizards
- Iguanas and chameleons

FAMILY

- Side-necked turtles
- African side-necked turtles
- Side-necked river turtles

- Pig-nosed turtles
- Snapping turtles
- Central American river turtles
- Sea turtles
- Leatherback turtles
- Pond turtles
- Eurasian pond turtles
- American mud turtles
- Tortoises
- Softshell turtles
- Big-headed turtles

- Boas
- Pythons
- Dwarf boas
- Split-jawed boas
- Asian sunbeam snakes
- Neotropical sunbeam snakes
- Dwarf pipesnakes
- Shield-tailed snakes
- Red pipesnakes
- Asian pipesnakes

- Colubrids
- Elapids
- Vipers
- Filesnakes
- Stiletto snakes

- Early blindsnakes
- Threadsnakes
- Blindsnakes

- Eyelid geckos
- Geckos
- Southwest Pacific geckos
- Flap-footed lizards

- Anguids
- Xenosaurs
- Beaded lizards
- Bornean earless monitors
- Monitor lizards

- Skinks
- Wall and sand lizards

- Iguanas
- Agamids
- Chameleons

- Alligators
- Crocodiles
- Gharials

Tuataras

GLOSSARY

abdomen The part of the body between the chest and the pelvic girdle (hips), often called the belly.

acrodont An animal that has teeth fused to the top of the jawbone.

adapted Changed in order to cope with the environment.

aestivation A state of dormancy similar to hibernation. Some reptiles are inactive in summer to avoid hot weather or drought or in winter to avoid cold weather and to conserve their energy.

aquatic Living in water.

autotomy The separation of a lizard's tail from its body.

camouflage Colours and patterns that let a reptile blend with its background.

carapace The protective upper shell of a turtle, made up of large, bony plates.

carnivorous An animal that hunts and eats other animals.

class A group of related organisms below a phylum but above an order.

cloaca A chamber into which the digestive, urinary and reproductive systems empty, opening to the outside through the anus.

clutch A set of eggs usually laid by one reptile and incubated at the same time.

constriction The method by which some snakes wrap their bodies around their prey, squeezing tighter and tighter until they crush or suffocate their victim.

courtship Behaviour between a male and female animal before they mate.

dislocate To force a bone out of its correct position.

diurnal Active during the day rather than at night.

ectothermic A term describing animals that cannot control their own body temperature, but take on the temperature of their environment.

egg tooth A temporary baby tooth that reptiles have at the tip of their snouts, used to break through the leathery eggshell.

embryo An early stage of a vertebrate's life before it is born.

evolution A process of change that takes place over a long period of time.

gestation The length of pregnancy, from fertilization to birth.

gizzard Part of the stomach that contains small stones, which are used to grind down the food into a paste before being digested.

habitat The natural environment or home of a plant or animal.

herbivore An animal that eats plants.

incubate To keep eggs warm, at the right temperature for development.

invertebrates Animals that do not have a backbone, for example insects and snails.

mammal An animal that is covered in hair and has a constant body temperature.

metabolism The chemical processes occurring within a living cell or organism that are necessary for the maintenance of life.

GLOSSARY

migration A regular journey between two different places at certain times of year.

moulting The process by which reptiles grow a new skin under the one they have, eventually replacing the old skin with the new.

nocturnal Active at night.

omnivore An animal that eats both animals and plants.

order A group of related organisms, positioned below a class and above a family.

pectoral girdle Bones that make up the shoulders.

pelvic girdle Bones that make up the hips.

phylum Main division of a kingdom, ranking above a class.

placenta An organ that develops in some female animals during pregnancy and which connects the mother to the developing young.

plastron The underside of a turtle shell, made up of nine bony plates.

poaching Illegal hunting.

predator An animal that catches and kills other animals for food.

prehensile Adapted for seizing, grasping, or holding, especially by wrapping around an object.

prey An animal that is caught and killed by a predator.

rainforest Dense forests found in tropical areas near to the Equator.

retina Part of the eye on which the light falls. The retina contains many light-sensitive cells.

scales A covering of plate-like structures on reptiles that provides protection from predators.

sp. An abbreviation for 'species', used as part of the Latin name for animals where the exact species is unknown.

spectacle scale A transparent scale that covers and protects the eye.

spur A small bony outgrowth.

streamlined Having a smooth outline or shape that slips easily through the water.

suffocate To stop an animal from breathing.

superfamily An intermediate group between a suborder and a family.

temperate A moderate climate that lacks extremes in temperature.

terrestrial Living on the ground.

translucent Almost transparent.

tropical Parts of the world that lie either side of the Equator, which usually have a hot, wet climate.

uncinate Something that is bent at the end like a hook.

venom The poisonous secretion of an animal, used to kill prey or as a defence against predators.

vertebrate An animal that has a backbone, for example fish, amphibians, reptiles, birds and mammals.

viviparous Able to give birth to live offspring.

webbed feet Having skin connecting the toes, which is helpful for swimming.